No Gifts, Please!

By Carrie Huber

This book is dedicated to
Alyssa, Hailey and Thomas because I have always
wanted you to have more in life than just MORE.

Contents

Memories > Monetary

What are we teaching our children today? Having a big house, nice car, lots of toys: Is that what's important? All over the country, more people are in debt and for what? It is time to teach our children what the true meaning of a party is: to be together. Many parents struggle and hem and haw about "No gifts, please." It is hard to come up with a viable alternative that people will actually participate in…Until now.

Here is a party planning book that will make the party easier, less expensive, MORE FUN, and will leave you and your child *feeling more* with *less stuff.*

Explore some ideas of how to take the emphasis off the presents, presents, presents and put the focus on PRESENCE.

Reality Check! Think back to your childhood. What do you remember? Yes, they are called MEMORIES. You do not likely remember the stuff; you remember the times you had, the friends, the laughing, and the moments. If you look into your photo album, what are the pictures of? What stories do you tell when you relive moments to your children?

So, why are we filling our own children up with stuff and watering down the moments? It is time to stop.

It is birthday time. What messages are you sending your child? Do you want your child to be the center of attention on his/her special, fun-filled day?

Or do you want your child to have a pile of more stuff at the end of a hectic, expensive day?

A birthday party can become overwhelming. The child opens and opens; gifts start to pile. The kids play with them once and toss them in the corner with the other seldom-used toys.

It is time for a party. What do you do? There is an endless supply of venues that are more than willing to market to your child and your child's friends. You start the ball rolling and end up with a party beyond your means, plans, and desires. A party that is *more than* what you want: more money, more time and more gifts. You were hoping for a party that was inexpensive, fun, personal, and meaningful. It is not too late to be the leader of change for the better. The following pages will put you on a path to making a birthday more than a party by making it a celebration of memories.

The ultimate goal of this book is to change the focus so that the gifts are actually contributions to the FUN and activity of the party, not just more stuff. Let's create a birthday celebration that the child will remember for the fun, activities, and being with friends. Anything your child can help with will enhance the experience for him or her, as well as fuel the momentum to get the birthday child excited for the party. If the birthday child has some part in the planning, you will have a better chance of avoiding the "no gift" let-down that your child might experience after the party.

Having a party with *no gifts* is seemingly impossible with the world we live in today. With the expectations in our society of always bringing a gift, it takes time to get used to coming to a party without a gift. After the first *no gift* party, those who attend will see that the gift does not make the party. You will be forever thankfully known as the one who finally broke the cycle.

Parties for All

Some of the parties in this book offer an option to ease you into the transition. A theme can help you focus on one collective gift that your child really wants and can be a step in the right direction.

Each party provides different options ("For Everyone," "For the Risk Taker" and "For the Very Daring") depending on your level of security in the idea of "No gifts, please."

For Everyone means just that. It is hanging a little on the safe edge but moving toward the idea of *no gifts*. The options for guests are simple, easy and straight forward. Most guests will feel better if you give them suggestions of what to bring such as something the birthday child will enjoy and won't already have. Included with each party theme is a list of items your guests can bring. I would suggest giving each guest a couple options but asking for them to respond with what they are bringing to make sure you have what you need.

For the Risk Taker means you are ready to step out on the limb a little further. You fully support the idea and are ready and willing to challenge your friends and guests, asking them to stretch their thinking and change the trend.

For the Very Daring means ideas to really shake it up. They are challenging the traditional thought of what a party should be, but that is the whole point.

The parties have themes and ideas that are flexible. The goal is to open your creative side and for this book to help you along. The parties presented here offer a good way to start, but, once you get the hang of it, go with your gut and have FUN!

Animal Lover Party

Fun Party Activities

For Everyone

Give each guest a list of a couple items to add to the vet clinic that will be open for the party. On each invitation, suggest a few items party guests can give to the birthday child. Some ideas are listed below. If you are really catching on to the whole "No gifts, please" concept and would rather the guests not bring anything for your house, then ask them to bring their own stuffed animal and each of them can take turns being the vet. The healed and bandaged animals will all return to their proper homes after the party.

Ideas for what the guests can bring: band-aids, gauze, child doctor set with stethoscope, pet leashes, little blankets, little pet beds for the stuffed animals, thermometer, doctor coat, toy shot, stuffed animals (if you think you need more), a jar for pretend medicine (such as raisins, fruit snacks, or crackers that can be given to the "sick" patient). If people are resisting your "no gifts" policy, encourage them to wrap any items they are bringing to the party.

For the Risk Taker

If guests would like to get the birthday child something, ask them to donate money or certain items to a local animal shelter. They could even wrap up some items for the birthday child to open and then donate to the shelter. Give them options of what animal shelter or place the birthday child would prefer. Having your child pick the charity will increase his or her excitement.

When the guests arrive, have them play vet on the birthday child's stuffed animals. Getting the birthday child a doctor coat so they can wear it and feel more like a real veterinarian adds to the party theme. Make paper plate animal masks. All you will need is paper plates, construction paper for ears, marker or crayons to decorate and an elastic strap to hold them on to the children's heads.

For the Very Daring
Take the party to a local animal shelter. Call ahead to make sure you are welcome and to plan any necessary details with the shelter. Decorate pencil boxes and have children bring items like dog treats, leashes, chew toys, etc. to give to the animal shelter. The shelter should be able to provide you with ideas on what will work for them and their animals. You can even make homemade dog treats with your guests before going to the shelter. Ask the shelter in advance for approval and find an easy recipe. Recipes for dog treats can be as simple as baby food and flour mixed together.

Party Favors

For Everyone
Decorate band-aids; the kids can decorate them with markers and take them home. Be sure to buy a lot because kids color the band-aids fast – just as fast as a band-aid heals a little wound. The kids could decorate the band-aids first before playing vet and then use them on their stuffed animals.

For the Risk Taker
Take pictures of the enthusiastic kids playing vet. Have the children decorate an animal themed frame to use when you provide the picture after the party. This can also be used as a thank you card.

For the Very Daring
Talk to the shelter to see if they have stickers or something to give to each child. Make a button saying that they helped animals today. If you do not have a button maker, ask around; a friend might have one, or you may be able to have the buttons made ahead of time at a local office supply store.

Make animal magnets by using cutout pictures from magazines, glue, and bottle caps with a magnet attached to the back. The kids can make the buttons or magnets themselves in order to increase their level of fun and involvement.

Games to Play
This is a good party to incorporate games along with the party activity and favor. Games that can be played:
Doggy, doggy where is my bone?
Duck, duck, goose
What time is it, Mr. Fox?
Pin the tail on the (*animal of choice*)
(Be creative. You can change any of the games above to fit the child's favorite animal, for example "What time is it, Ms. Monkey?")

Play music during the party:
"Chicken Dance"
"Who Let the Dogs Out?"

Invitations
Take a picture of your child dressed as an animal or find a picture of any animal to use as the invitation with the party details on the back.

Write the birthday information on a strip of paper and attach it to a pet related item such as leash, collar, or a treat in the shape of a dog bone for the child.

Cake and Food Ideas
Make the cake look like the birthday child's favorite animal. To make it easy on you, bake a sheet cake and purchase plastic animals to put on top for the birthday child to keep. Decorate it with green icing for grass or blue for water, depending on the animals you have available.

Make little cupcakes with animal faces on them. You can use round cookies for ears, licorice strings for whiskers, and small round candy pieces for eyes. To simplify it, put an animal cracker on top of a green cupcake.

Make a sheet cake and cut out the cake to look like the animal. Print a large picture of the animal and cut around it if needed. Then decorate with icing to make it look like the animal.

Art Enthusiast Party

Fun Party Activities

For Everyone

Ask guests to bring various watercolor paints. Cut watercolor paper into shapes, or you can use coffee filters. Let the guests paint the shapes. The paints become the gift, and the watercolor designs are the party favors.

Ideas for what the guests can bring: Various watercolor paints, paint brushes, paint smocks, construction paper, coffee filters, canvas panels, white tee shirts, easel, art set, sketch book, oil pastels, and supplies for whatever type of art your child enjoys.

For the Risk Taker

Drape a large white sheet over a clothes line, over a fence or attached to a wall (or other hard surface). Spray the sheet with a hose to get it wet and give the guests a variety of painting utensils: spray bottles filled with paint, brushes, leaves, sticks, branches, feathers, hands. You can even use matchbox cars to paint with by rolling the wheels in paint, especially for the boys. Let the imaginative children create their own work of art on the sheet. You can even spray it again to rinse the paint off and let them create a new masterpiece.

For the Very Daring

Purchase a large canvas. Have each guest wear a white tee shirt (or have someone bring these as their party contribution "gift"). Prepare five or more large containers of different colored paint. Give each guest a paintbrush and let him or her "throw" the paint on the canvas (best if you can do this outside). The kids are creating the birthday gift and their party favor at the same time, since they will likely get a lot of paint on those shirts that serve as a cover-up as well as being their party favor. Using their fingers and hands to finish painting their shirts can add to the fun as well. T-shirts are a good idea that can be incorporated into any party theme.

Party Favors
For Everyone
Watercolor shapes that each guest painted.

For the Risk Taker
Have some extra watercolor shapes for the guests to take home or give them a set of paint colors and paper. For the final project, try using permanent paint. You can give each guest a plain tee shirt to wear during this project, and that can be the gift to take home.

For the Very Daring
While the guests throw paint, encourage them to get a little on their shirts. The nice paint-thrown shirts are the party favor.

Invitations
If people are resisting your "no gifts" policy, encourage them to wrap whatever they are bringing to the party.

If you are mailing them: Have your child paint on a big sheet of paper. When the paint is dry cut the paper into shapes to make the invitations and write the party information on the back.

If you are hand delivering them: A paintbrush with the invitation tied to it.

Cake and Food Ideas
Color palette: Bake a 13 x 9 inch cake. Cut it in a circle, oval, or a solid 8 shape. Frost it all one color, probably white, and put circles of other colors in a row to make it look like a paint holder. Stick a clean (preferably new) paintbrush on the cake as the finishing touch. An additional option would be to create an edible paintbrush using a pretzel rod and licorice strands at the end.

Decorate cupcakes in all sorts of different colors. Easy and simple you could also add a mini paintbrush made with a mini pretzel and licorice on the end, on top of each cupcake.

Have the birthday child create a piece of art; transfer it to rice paper or ask a bakery to put it on a cake.

At this party for your artist, it might be a fun idea to make a blank cake and let the guests do the decorating. The frosting and icing is their "paint" on the canvas of the cake. Be sure to take a picture of the final masterpiece.

Cookies or cupcakes the kids can "paint" with frosting and eat.

Fruit pizza the kids can make. Be sure to pick all sorts of colored fruits. You can use pre-made sugar cookie for the crust that is cut into circles and cooked ahead of time. Have a sauce ready for the kids to spread on the crust - a cream cheese or yogurt sauce will work well. Then kids top the cake with the fruit. Food *is* art, so, thematically, this works, too. If you choose to have the kids make the food, you could also do a real pizza, nachos, or sandwiches for letting the kids use their creativity and giving them independence to make their own food.

15

Baking Party

Fun Party Activities

For Everyone

Select, or have the birthday child select, something to make at the party: e.g. brownies, a cake, pizza, play dough, etc. Figure out what items and ingredients you may need so that you can include them in the invitation and guests can bring them to the party. Have a big table ready to get messy once everyone arrives. The kids can use the "gifts" they brought to make whatever item the birthday child picked.

Ideas for what the guests can bring: spatula, muffin pan, mixing bowl, apron, cookbooks, timer, sugar, flour, pizza pan, baking pan, measuring cups and spoons, milk, eggs, towels, clean-up wipes, recipe cards, silicone baking cups, non-stick baking mat, cake decorating set, baking rack, spices, and seasonings. The list could go on and should be customized, depending on what you are making.

For the Risk Taker

Ask each person to bring an ingredient of their own choice or an ingredient the birthday child enjoys. Once everyone arrives, take inventory and have the guests come up with something to make. You might be able to make more than one dish. Be prepared to supplement from your own kitchen.

You could ask each person to bring ingredients for their favorite food to make, and each person can create their own. Have the birthday child taste test to have him/her pick a favorite which creates another party activity: baking contest.

For the Very Daring

Have those at the party prepare food and take it to a local shelter or to someone less fortunate.

Party Favors

For Everyone

Have a batch of wooden spoons in the middle of the table. While the food is cooking, let the kids decorate the spoons to take home. Have paint, sharpies, yarn, fabric, glue, googly eyes, pipe cleaners and other craft supplies on hand to encourage all sorts of creativity. Maybe this will inspire you to come up with your own theme: a clean-up party.

Another item to decorate would be an apron; have the guests paint their own apron to keep.

For the Risk Taker

Give each person a sample of what they created to take home and share. You could have some durable paper plates or plastic food containers that the kids can decorate while the food cooks, and then they can take the food home in what they made. Empty shoeboxes lined with aluminum foil would work well for this too. Leaving out markers, stickers and other craft supplies would be useful in case they choose to decorate.

For the Very Daring

Provide a picture of them baking or giving the food away to someone less fortunate. While the items are baking, you could have each kid make a recipe card holder.

Ideas for holder: Use a mini flower pot with clay in the bottom, stick a wooden craft stick in the clay and glue a clothespin to the stick. Make sure the clothespin opens at the top to hold an index card with the recipe. Have some of the birthday child's favorite recipes out for the kids to take home with them and inspire them to cook more at home.

Games to play

A fun game to play would be to put baking items into brown lunch bags and have the guests close their eyes, feel what is inside the bag and try to guess what it is.

17

Blindfold the guests and have them taste food. See who can correctly identify all the food. Having about five to ten options should be good. Check about guests allergies before deciding the food.

Relay with oranges - two teams pass an orange in between them without using hands. They can use elbows, knees, necks, or any other body parts.

Egg toss contest outside. Each team consists of two players, lined up tossing a raw egg back and forth until it breaks. The last team to keep the egg whole wins.

Invitations

If people are resisting your "no gifts" policy, encourage them to wrap whatever they are bringing to the party.

If you are mailing them or hand delivering them: Put the invitation on a recipe card with a recipe that the birthday child enjoys.

Cake and Food Ideas

If you are willing and able, you could have the party guests bake the birthday cake.

If the party does not allow for time to bake and decorate, you could have it baked ahead of time and let them decorate it.

Use whatever food you are preparing to serve to your guests at the party.

It would be a good idea for this party to have fruits and vegetables for the kids to eat during the party.

Baseball/Softball Party

Fun Party Activities

For Everyone

Ask each guest to bring baseball equipment (substitute softball for baseball as needed). Give suggestions so you don't end up with 20 baseballs. You could even write three different suggestions on each card to make sure that you don't have duplicates.

Ideas for what the guests can bring: soft baseball, hard baseball, wiffle ball and bat, soft and hard bats, bases, a t-ball set, mitt, batting gloves, batting helmet, catchers gear, pouches of gum, sunflower seeds.

After everyone arrives, have the child open the gifts and go outside to play a game with the whole party. The party could take place at a local baseball diamond or park. After the game, the guests can sign the ball to give to the birthday child.

For the Risk Taker

Have the party at a local baseball diamond. You might have to check about reserving it. Some parks have grills available or bring your own to cook the food for the party. Ask each guest to bring their own baseball mitt and a bat if they have one to share. Play a game of baseball. Take lots of pictures.

For the Very Daring

Take the party to a baseball game. Minor league games are accommodating to young children and are very reasonable.

Party Favors

For Everyone

Purchase baseball hats at a fabric store. Make sure to get light colors and have a table set up for the kids to paint the hats. If you find that the hats cost too much and t-shirts are cheaper, have the kids make baseball shirts. If you get two different colors, they could use them for team divisions in the game. Fabric markers might be a good option because you don't have to wait for them to dry.

For the Risk Taker
Buy some baseballs and give one to each kid. Have a clean ball that each guest can sign with permanent marker. Set up a table and let the kids decorate their baseballs with paint or markers. Paint may take some time to dry, so be sure to do this craft before the game.

Invitations
If you are mailing them or hand delivering them: Make the invitation in the shape of a circle. Trace a lid from a jar to help you. On the front, turn it into a baseball by adding the laces and on the back write the information.

Take a picture of your child in a baseball hat, holding a bat. Make it look like a baseball card with the party information on the back.

Cake and Food Ideas
Take two round glass bowls. Depending on the size of the cake you want, big or little will work. For my son's 1st birthday, I used little bowls about the size of cupcakes and made each guest their own baseball cake. Be sure to put the glass bowls on a baking sheet. When the cake is done, frost the flat sides and stick them together to form the ball shape. You might need to cut a small slice of cake off the bottom, so the cake won't roll. Frost the ball with white frosting; you may need a little extra icing on top to give the cake a more rounded effect. Take black or red gel and make the laces to look like a baseball. Another option is to use red rope licorice and create the laces that way.

Make a sheet cake and decorate it to look like a baseball diamond, using green and brown frosting. Add some plastic baseball guys on the top for the birthday child to keep.

Hot dogs are a great thing to serve at a baseball birthday party. Creating a baseball park theme is easy with food. Think of what you

might get at the ballpark: nachos, popcorn, peanuts, Cracker Jack, cotton candy. Serve the food in paper trays/bags or on paper plates like at the game.

Budding Photographer/Scrapbook Party

Fun Party Activities

For Everyone

Ask guests to bring some of their favorite pictures of themselves. Before the party, purchase a large frame (11 x 14 or larger). Have a table ready with scissors, ribbon, stickers, etc. Guests will fill the frame with the pictures they brought, and they can decorate the frame any way they want. Sectioning off the frame to give each guest responsibility and creative freedom over a portion will alleviate some arguments. This is a collaborative activity, so be sure to monitor and guide. At the end of the party, the birthday child has a great gift: the frame that everyone made. It will be a good idea to have some extra pictures of your own of the birthday child with his/her invited friends.

If your child would like a camera, this would be a great chance to suggest to the guests that they could donate money to the birthday child for a new camera. Get a small box; turn it into a camera and cut a slit on the top for money to go in.

Have a picture frame matted so that the guests can sign the matting as another "gift." Then, use a photo from the party to complete the frame for the child.

Ideas for what guests can bring depending on the party: scrapbook paper, disposable cameras, stickers, ribbon, glue, tape, scissors, scrapbook box, buttons, paper in shapes, stencils, brown paper bags, wooden craft sticks, yarn, hole puncher, craft supplies, more paper and more stickers.

For the Risk Taker

Ask each guest to bring pictures and one scrapbook item as the gift. At the party, each guest will make his or her own little scrapbook. You will need brown paper bags, a hole punch, yarn, scissors, and other various scrapbook supplies. Put about 3-4 brown paper lunch bags together horizontally, fold them in half, and punch two holes in the closed end. Put yarn through the two holes and tie a bow. This makes a nice, little, sturdy scrapbook for each guest. Depending on the ages of your guests, decide how much assembling of the bag scrapbooks the guests can do. You can have the basic book ready or they can create it as a party activity. The guests can decorate the scrapbooks with their own pictures and share the contributed scrapbook supplies. If the guests don't have enough pictures, they can create the pages and add pictures later.

Have a supply of disposable cameras or borrow enough digital cameras for teams of guests. Create a photo scavenger hunt and have the guests work to get the most items in the fewest shots. A photo scavenger hunt can be modified and fun for all ages. For the younger ones, they can take pictures of toys, an animal outside, flowers, colors, kids upside down, a bag filled with as much trash as you can collect, etc. For older kids, a member on the team in a tree, a team member sitting on a specific item like a rock, a creative group photo, etc.

For the Very Daring
If your child has a camera, or can borrow yours, have a photo shoot. Ask each guest to be ready for the red carpet. Have some make-up and hair accessories available for the guests to get themselves glamorous. If your guests are older children, have some of your dresses or dress-up clothes out if they would like to wear them, or ask them to bring some fancy clothes. Have a background for your child to take some pictures. Let your child play photographer for his or her friends, or each child could take turns. You could do a location photo shoot too.

Party Favors
For Everyone
Get each guest a little frame to take home. Some places have inexpensive wood frames that the kids can decorate. Have the kids make some simple frames, using cardboard and fabric, wooden craft sticks, or even foam. The kids can embellish the frames using items such as feathers, stones, stickers, paint, googly eyes and foam letters.

For the Risk Taker
The scrapbook they make is the gift they take home. I did this party, and the kids loved it; they all went home wanting to scrapbook more.

For the Very Daring
Memories! Laughter! You can even have the kids make a frame and print some pictures from the photo shoots, if you have the right printer at home. Or print them after the party to give out with thank you cards.

Games to play
Photo scavenger hunt – described above as an activity but could be turned into a game.

What is wrong with the picture? Before the party, have your child create a couple scenes. The child can take a picture of the scene and then remove some items or change something about the picture. Snap the picture again. Have the child do about five different picture scenes, and the guests have to identify the differences.

Invitations
If people are resisting your "no gifts" policy, encourage them to wrap whatever they are bringing to the party.

If you are mailing them or hand delivering them: Make the invitation look like a camera.

Have a picture of the birthday child as the invitation.

Have the birthday child make the invitations similar to a scrapbook page.

Cake and Food Ideas
Camera Cake – nice, easy, rectangle cake, just decorate with icing to look like a camera, flash and lens.

Scrapbook cake - make a sheet cake. Let it cool and decorate with colorful frosting to look like scrapbook paper. Print up pictures on paper or rice paper to decorate the cake like a scrapbook page.

Hollywood-style glamorous photo shoot with cheese, crackers, fruit, veggies, tiny sandwiches, plastic champagne glasses, and anything you can cut up into bite-size hors d'oeuvres.

Decorating Bonus
Make sure your house is ready for this party with a red carpet, stars on the wall, and pictures of the birthday child.

Building Block Party

Fun Party Activities

<u>For Everyone</u>

Ask each guest to bring some building blocks for the birthday child to keep. Make sure to add that they can bring all sorts of different pieces. Encourage the guests to bring in blocks they have at home; just some pieces that they may not need anymore. Or, if they prefer, they can pick up a new set but keep it under a set dollar amount. Once all the pieces are together, the birthday child will have a great collection. Building blocks are great for all ages. I know grown men who would love building blocks for their birthday.

Ideas for what the guests can bring: building blocks from home, new building block sets that are small, new building block people (they are sold individually now). Give each guest a plastic bag to fill with a certain color of building block.

<u>For the Very Daring</u>

When you send invitations, just ask the guests to bring their creativity. At this party you will need to supply a big box of building blocks. After all the guests arrive, have the building blocks readily available. Then ask each guest to create something for the birthday child. It can be about the child, what he/she likes, a memory that guest had with the birthday child, a game, etc. Give them a time limit to work on the creation. Let the birthday child join in this timed fun. Have each child display and explain what he or she has made. Depending on the age of the guests, the birthday child can pick the favorite and give the creator a prize. Or the birthday child can give each guest an award in categories such as most creative, funniest, craziest, biggest, smallest, most colorful, etc. The awards could be certificates, medals or something the birthday child creates at the party.

Party Favors

For Everyone

Buy or look for a bunch of different building block people. Have them separated so the guests can mix and match, create and take a person home as a party favor.

For the Very Daring

Have the guests take their creations home. Or the birthday child keeps the creations but takes a picture of the kids with what they created. Send the photos as the thank you notes.

Invitations

If people are resisting your "no gifts" policy, encourage them to wrap whatever they are bringing to the party.

If you are mailing them or hand delivering them: Make the paper look like a building block.

Use mailing labels to print out the party information and stick the label to a giant building block.

Cake and Food Ideas

You can make any regular cupcakes and on top put one piece of a building block set. The guests can keep what was on their cupcake. Clean the pieces before placing them on the cupcakes, or put some clear wrap around the bottom of piece to help keep it clean.

If you would like one big cake on which to write "Happy Birthday," make a rectangular cake and lightly frost the top. Cut off the top of six cupcakes, and turn the cupcake bottoms upside down on the top of the iced part of the rectangular cake. Make two equal rows of cupcakes on the rectangular portion of the cake. Frost over the entire cake (cupcake bottoms now included) with your child's favorite color. The final result will look like one large building block piece.

Start with an iced sheet cake and top with a completed building block set, finished by yourself or your child. With this party, I used a new building block construction set that I put together and placed on the cake that resembled a road. (It was for his 2nd birthday, so he was a little young to make it himself.) If you go with this option, place some foil on the bottom of the blocks so cake and frosting do not get stuck in the blocks.

With this creative party, have ingredients ready for the kids to make their own sandwich, pasta, or pizza. The kids will be *building* their own meal.

Car Party

Fun party activities

For Everyone

Ask guests to bring a small, toy car of their choice. For the party, prepare a miniature city for the kids to play in with the cars they bring. You and the birthday child can design and construct the city prior to the party. WARNING: Building the city with you may be what your child remembers most! Let your imagination run! Use crepe paper hanging from a stick and call it a car wash. Empty juice boxes, milk cartons, and shoe boxes are excellent for city buildings. Use wrapping paper tubes cut in half and raised on end to make a slanted race track. Make sure to include a gas station. This can easily be made with a small box, a string attached to the box and a paperclip on the end of the string to make the pump.

Ideas for what the guests can bring: tiny cars, crepe paper, old cereal boxes, wrapping paper tubes, paper towels tubes, oatmeal containers, yarn, ribbon, empty cartons of juice, paint, buttons, soda bottles tops, balloons, straws, and wood scraps.

For the Risk Taker

Ask each guest to bring a car. You supply the material, and *they* come up with the city (see above). You must be patient and brave to let the kids create the city. You could leave some pictures of buildings to give them ideas or instructions if you found some for how to make the buildings. The kids will have a blast and surprise everyone with what they can come up with. If you do not have enough recycled items to make the city, you can ask for guests to supply items that will be used for it.

You can also buy a big canvas and some paint. Make sure the guests come ready to get dirty or have some extra clothes. Ask the kids at the party to make a city on the canvas. When it is done, the birthday child gets to keep it. Remind them they need roads and buildings and houses. If they are younger, you could draw everything and have them paint what you drew.

Another idea is to get a canvas for each child attending the party. Put some paint on plates and place an old car in each paint color. Each child can run the car through the paint and then drive on his/her canvas to create a masterpiece (especially for the younger kids). It will not be a city but will be a great painting.

For the Very Daring
Have the kids design their own cars and race them. You supply what they will need, such as small pieces of wood, nuts, nails, and other hardware. You can make soap box cars, eraser cars, or wooden cars. Ask the birthday child what he/she would like to use. Make sure to have a track ready or use an outdoor slide. When they are done constructing their cars, they can race.

Party Favors
For Everyone
Have the birthday child give a piece of the city to each friend. Remind the child that you can always build another city together. Make sure the birthday child keeps one as well.

Mini play cars are reasonable and something small that kids love to play with. You can always get each kid a new car as the party favor.

For the Risk Taker
If you have each guest create a building or painting, they can keep the piece they made.

For the Very Daring
They get to keep the car they designed and constructed.

Invitations
If people are resisting your "no gifts" policy, encourage them to wrap whatever they are bringing to the party.

If you are mailing them or hand delivering them: cut the invitations into circles to make them look like a steering wheel or tire. Car shaped invitations work well too.

Cake and Food Ideas

Make a square cake. Cut part of it off and add it on the top middle to look like a car. Bake two small round cakes cut in half for tires or use circular cookies. For this party I added a picture of my son, making it look like he was driving the car cake.

Make a brownie in the shape of the age of the birthday child. Add a yellow line down the middle and some play cars on each side to make it look like a road. Each guest can keep a car as a party favor.

Make little subs and turn them into cars. Cucumber slices attached to the side of the sub with toothpicks make great wheels.

Dress-Up Party

Fun Party Activities
<u>For Everyone</u>
Have each guest bring one dress (new or old - whichever you prefer). Have a big trunk (box) ready, and they can add their dress to the trunk. If this is a party for boys and girls, ask each of them to bring in an old Halloween costume. The kids at the party can dress up and show off. Have fun with it; turn the lights off and use a flashlight as a spotlight on them when they walk out all dressed up. Create a runway for the models by laying down a blanket or rug. Depending on the age, the kids could dress up and put on a show that you can record.

Ideas for what the guests can bring: dresses, costumes, hats, feather boas, necklaces, shoes, nail polish, hair pieces, clip on earrings, bracelets, wigs, makeup.

<u>For the Risk Taker</u>
Ask each person to bring in old jewelry that they no longer want. The guests can put on the jewelry and get fancy for the party. If you are daring enough, have a nail painting station and paint the guests fingernails or "do" their hair for them.

<u>For the Very Daring</u>
You could ask each person to come dressed up and have the kids put on a play or dance at the party.

Ask each guest to bring a nail polish color, and each girl can polish another girl's nails.

Each guest can bring in hair and makeup items. After everyone arrives, turn the lights off and have the girls do makeovers in the dark. It may not be the prettiest makeover, but it will be a lot of fun!

Party Favors
For Everyone
Have a basket of your jewelry ready for the kids to play with during the party. If you do not want to give yours away, you can buy some cheap costume jewelry or ask people for their old jewelry as a party donation. When they leave, guests each select a piece to take home.

For the Risk Taker
If you have a table set up for the party, have the guests' place settings ready, including cups with their name on it. They can take the cup home with them. If you are having a hard time finding special cups, such as teacups, then look for cheap white coffee mugs and use those. You can write on it with permanent marker; just remind guests to hand wash only.

For the Very Daring
Have the kids make a jewelry box. You can use a cheap plastic pencil case or a small cardboard box. Have stickers, glitter, foam letters, or even some unmatched jewelry pieces available for them to glue onto their creations.

Games to Play
Fishing for outfits – On index cards or small pieces of paper, write different articles of clothing you have on hand. Put a paper clip on a group of them (maybe three) that would make a funny outfit together. Place the groups of cards in a box. Turn a stick, string, and magnet into a fishing pole. With the pile of clothes next to the cards, have the kids take turns fishing out an outfit and putting it on. Examples: apron, scarf, and boots. Or dress, oven mitt, and heels.

Toilet paper dress – Separate kids into groups. Give each group a toilet paper roll, some ribbon, and some fabric pieces you may have. Let each group design an outfit on someone with the materials provided.

Invitations

If people are resisting your "no gifts" policy, encourage them to wrap whatever they are bringing to the party.

If you are mailing them or hand delivering them: Attach an invitation to a piece of jewelry. Find cheap beaded necklaces and make a label containing the important party information to attach to them as the invitations.

Cake and Food Ideas

Make a rectangular cake and turn it into a jewelry box. Decorate the outside of the cake and lay some wax paper on top. Place play jewelry on top of the wax paper. Kids can keep the jewelry on their piece or just stick candy jewelry right on the icing. If you want to add a lid for the cake jewelry box, make a thin, large cookie so it will be sturdier. Then, hold it "open" at an angle on top of the cake by supporting it with toothpicks or popsicle sticks.

Turn a cupcake into a tea cup with frosting and a wafer or other cookie cut in half and stuck in the side for the handle.

Have a table ready for a tea party: tiny sandwiches, mini burritos, pizza rolls, chicken nuggets, or any little finger food. Also, decorate the table with a white tablecloth made of paper that the guests can write and draw on. The autographed tablecloth is a great gift for the birthday child.

Game Night Party

Fun Party Activities
<u>For Everyone</u>
Have each guest bring a favorite game to play with the group. Make it clear that ALL games will be played during the party. This could be a new game the guest would like to give to the birthday child or one of his or her favorite games to share and take home. This is a great party to invite the whole family, not just the kids.

Ideas for what the guests can bring: games, dice, cards, a dish to pass for snacking on while playing games.

<u>For the Risk Taker</u>
Have each guest bring a favorite game that they will be donating to the party. All games will be played and each person will go home with a new (used) game. Very much like a white elephant party, but the birthday boy/girl will actually get to play with each "gift" brought to the party. And that is what they want to do anyway! Let the birthday child have first choice of games. Then the guests can draw numbers for the order in which they will pick a remaining game to take home.

<u>For the Very Daring</u>
Have each guest bring a favorite game to play and meet at a local senior center or children's hospital. Have the birthday child select a location and contact them ahead of time to arrange the details. Play games with the people who are at the location of your choice. Be sure to have the kids split up and play with new people.

Party Favors
<u>For Everyone</u>
Give each guest a deck of cards to take home; everyone can use more cards. Include the rules for some games to play with the deck of cards, possibly the games that your child enjoys playing.

For the Risk Taker
Each guest can take home a new (used) game that another guest brought and played at the party. You may want to have some extra games available to allow all guests, even those selecting at the end, a few choices.

For the Very Daring
Take a picture of the group playing games at the location of choice. Pictures are a gift that the guests can always look at to remember the party. Have your child make a little album for each guest, which you can give to them after the party. With this party, try and help the kids at the party remember how they helped the world to be a better place. That can be a magnificent gift by itself.

Invitations
If people are resisting your "no gifts" policy, encourage them to wrap whatever they are bringing to the party.

If you are mailing them or hand delivering them: Use a picture of a game board and shrink it to be the front of the invitation with the information on the back.

Attach the party information onto a game piece or large dice.

Cake and Food Ideas
Duplicate a gameboard. For example, make a square checkerboard design for the top of the cake. You could even add some real checkers on top or turn some candy circles into the game pieces.

For this party, I created a candy game cake (with the help of a friend), and it was fun! With the game board as a guide, I used all sorts of candy to duplicate it. There was a lot of candy decorating it, and the kids really enjoyed the finished product. It also made me realize you can just put some candy on top of a cake and call it good. The more candy the better. This could be a good cake to do right after Halloween!

Cupcakes, with a clean, used game piece on top.

This is a great party for appetizers. During the game playing or breaks from the games, the guests can enjoy the food options. If this is a party for the whole family or maybe the kids are a little older, a potluck will help make the party simpler and allows people to contribute something to the party.

Gardening Enthusiast Party

Fun Party Activities

For Everyone

Use seeds or small plants to create mini greenhouses. Here are some ideas:

Cut a 2-liter bottle in half. Fill the bottom with dirt. Insert the seed or small plant into the dirt. Sprinkle with water. Fit the bottle back together and use tape to secure it in one piece.

Pre-make, or have guests make, window boxes. Decorate with stickers, markers, or paint. Fill bottom with dirt, plant, and water.

Plant individual gardens in terra cotta pots or plastic cups. Decorate them with stickers, markers, or paint. Fill bottom with dirt, plant, and water.

Ideas for what the guests can bring: seeds, flowers, plants, dirt, shovels, gardening gloves, wood pieces, pine cones, 2-liter bottles, small bag of bulbs, watering can.

For the Risk Taker

Donate window boxes or pots made at the party to neighbors or a local retirement community.

Take the party a step further and have it at a local retirement community, so you can plant right on their grounds. Be sure to contact them in advance and have all your gardening supplies ready (such as extra dirt, the plants, hand shovels, trowels, rakes, etc.). Bring a picnic with you and, when everyone is done, sit down to have a bite.

For the Very Daring

Have each guest bring an outdoor plant of his or her choice. Be ready for variety. On the invitation, explain that the plant will be outside, so please select plants native or conducive to your climate: veggies, fruit, flowers, and even a tree if they wish. Set the guests to work on a plot of your land. Leave the designing to them. Make sure that you are ready for anything to happen. Resist the urge to jump in and direct or to fix it when they are done. Just let it grow; you might be surprised, and the kids will love it.

Party Favors
For Everyone
The mini greenhouses or planters they made.

The guests could make mini bird feeders for them to take home as well. Tie a string to a pinecone and cover it with peanut butter and birdseed.

For the Risk Taker
Make a picture frame that says "Thank you for helping" along with the date and the birthday child's name on it using paint or permanent marker. Send a picture from the party as the thank you card for them to put in the frame.

Give each child seeds to take home to plant. Maybe this is VERY daring as you've just given the guests' parents something to do.

For the Very Daring
Send them an update with the thank you cards on how the plants look. If, during the party, the kids planted fruit or vegetables and they are growing, have a picking party when they are ripe and ready. This party is a 2 for 1 deal. The kids will enjoy eating what they planted.

Find some gardening gloves that are plain. Have the kids decorate their own pair of gloves to take home.

Invitations
If people are resisting your "no gifts" policy, encourage them to wrap whatever they are bringing to the party.

If you are mailing them or hand delivering them: Cut out a terra cotta pot shape and fold a paper cut flower inside with the party information.

Hand out a bulb in a bag with the invitation attached. I did this for my child's first birthday as the thank you note and added "As you plant it and watch it grow, think of me as I grow each and every year."

Put the invitation inside gardening gloves.

Cake and Food Ideas
Dirt cups
Ingredients and Supplies:
2 cups milk
1 pkg. (4 serving size) Chocolate Instant Pudding
1 tub Whipped Topping thawed
15 Chocolate sandwich cookies, finely crushed
10 worm-shaped gummy snacks
10 small paper or plastic cups
Make pudding according to directions on box. Gently stir in whipped topping and ½ cup of the cookie crumbs. Spoon mixture into 10 paper or plastic cups; top with remaining cookie crumbs. Refrigerate at least 1 hour. Top with worm.

Garden Gate Cake
Ingredients and Supplies:
Pre-made pound cake (or make your own loaf)
Chocolate frosting
Green food coloring
One package lady fingers
Coconut flakes
Large gumdrops
Granulated sugar
Toothpicks
Wax Paper

41

Ice the top and sides of the cake with chocolate frosting. Cut the top of each ladyfinger into a point to resemble picket fence post. Gently press the pickets against the frosted sides of the loaf cake. In a bag, mix green food coloring with coconut flakes. Sprinkle now-green coconut flakes over top of the frosted cake to resemble grass. Sprinkle granulated sugar and one gum drop at a time onto wax paper. Use a rolling pin to flatten gumdrops to ¼ inch thick. Using kitchen scissors cut flattened gumdrops to resemble tulips. Insert toothpick stem into blossom. Plant each blossom into the top of the cake. Repeat for as many flowers as desired.

This is a great party for veggie and fruit trays. Add ranch, French onion, and caramel dip for finger food fun.

Mini ceramic planter

Golf Theme Party

Fun Party Activities
<u>For Everyone</u>
Make a mini golf course in your backyard. Recyclable materials work well and allow for much creativity. Involving your child will make it more fun and build memories which could be the BEST part of this party! Let your child come up with each hole. Depending on the age of your child, he/she could design it first on paper before creating the real course. Using materials already available around your house, make ramps, tunnels, and turns to create a small putt-putt course. For this party, you could use some plastic golf clubs or be creative and have the kids use bats, sticks, or even umbrellas.

Another option is to make a finger golf course (see photo on page 45) using cereal or cracker boxes – any shape and size will do. You'll need green felt, glue, marbles, toothpicks, construction paper and wooden craft sticks. You may want to cut a hole in the box before the party; when I did this for my son's birthday, it seemed to be the toughest part of the project. The hole can be anywhere on the biggest side of the box and should be a little bigger than your marble to be used as the golf ball. At the party, the kids can then cover the box with green felt and glue. You may want some hot glue on hand to help finish it off and make sure it will stick. You will either need to cut a hole in the felt to match up with the one on the box or cut the hole through the felt after it is covering the hole. Once the green felt is on, you can fence it in by gluing the wooden craft sticks around the outside edge of the box. Make sand traps using brown felt or water hazards using blue felt. Cut a small triangle out of construction paper and glue it onto the toothpick to use as a flagstick to mark the hole. I just did the green felt with my son when he was three years old, and he still loved to play with it several years later. The nice thing is that you can place the marble in the box and stand it up on a shelf for easy storage.

Ideas for what the guests can bring: golf club, golf ball, wooden ramps, pipes for the ball to go through, wrapping paper tubes cut in half, cereal boxes, oatmeal boxes.

For the Risk Taker
Ask each family to come up with their own putting hole: one hole per family. Let them know that they will have to bring the items needed for the hole and set it up at the party. When all the guests have arrived and set up their holes, everyone plays a round of putt-putt. If you don't feel comfortable asking each family to make the entire hole, you could also ask each person to bring some items that they think could be used for a putt-putt course and wrap them up as the gift. When the child is done opening the "gifts," the kids get to take all the items and make a putt-putt course to play on. Depending on the age of the children, you may need to help them. It is amazing what kids can come up with. If you are making the course during the party, make sure to have some of your own items you think may be useful for its creation. The items used to create the holes then serve as the party activities and the "gifts" for the birthday child who can then play putt-putt whenever he or she wishes.

Party Favors
For Everyone
The guests will be able to take home their completed finger golf crafts.

For the Risk Taker
Have golf balls for the kids to color. Permanent marker works the best, so have a well covered area for clean up. There are all sorts of colors of permanent markers; kids can make their golf balls very cool and unique. Acrylic paint can also be used. Provide a risk-free zone for creating, as there are bound to be spills. One method for handling this is to pour some of each color into paper bowls. The kids can roll the golf balls around in the paints. Have wax paper ready for them to place the golf balls on for the paint to dry. The paint will need some drying time that the markers do not.

Invitations

If people are resisting your "no gifts" policy, encourage them to wrap whatever they are bringing to the party.

If you are mailing them or hand delivering them: Make a paper invitation in the shape of a golf ball or golf club. Or make a mini club with a pipe cleaner and craft foam. Tie the invitation to the "club."

Cake and Food Ideas

Using the ball idea (see the baseball party), bake the cake in bowls and adhere it together with frosting. Make pockmarks (dimples) all over the white frosted ball to make it look like a golf ball.

Make a golf course. A rectangle cake with green frosting, some mounds (made from odd cake pieces) and a couple holes with flags makes a great golf course. If you are really creative, you can add trees using pretzel sticks and green candy, sand traps with brown frosting, water using blue frosting or blue jello, a golfer, golf cart, etc.

Meatballs would be a good fun meal for a golf party. You can have them plain and have different sauces for guests to sample. Along with them, have some green veggies or a salad.

45

Karaoke Party

You can adapt this party for the **Music Lover** without the karaoke part, for the **Rock Star**, and/or a **Sleepover Party.** Have a lip synching battle if kids are too nervous to sing.

Fun Party Activities
For Everyone
Ask that each guest make a CD or song list on an electronic device to bring to the party for the birthday child. It could be just one song or ten songs; they can pick. One of the songs they choose needs to be one they are willing to sing for everyone. At the party, every child will sing the song of their choice, with a group or alone. They can decide.

If you do not own a karaoke machine, have a CD player ready with an attached microphone or just a play microphone – kids can be loud enough without the speakers. If you do not have microphones, you can make some or have the kids grab something they think will work: a brush, the remote, a pen, whatever they can come up with at the spur of the moment. This might also reduce the amount of fighting over the microphone, and it can become a party game: vote for the most creative microphone choice. Another version of the party is to get a karaoke app. Have the birthday child pick all the songs for the party that he or she would like each friend to sing at the party. (For an alternative, ask that they send you their song ahead of time. You can download all of them and burn each child a CD, as the party favor. For some songs, you can download the Karaoke version.)

Have blank CDs ready on a table for the kids to decorate. They can make a great decoration on the wall or even as a coaster to put a cup on. Have paint, markers, beads, feathers, sequins, stickers, felt; be creative. You could even have pictures out for them to cut and glue on the CD. Add a pop can top or some type of hook glued to the back of the CD so the kids can hang them. Hot glue the part you pulled off the can to the back of the CD and make sure the tab is sticking out from the CD, if you choose to do it this way.

Get some materials you think would work to make a microphone. For my daughter's birthday, I used empty toilet paper tubes and foam balls, with felt and foil. If you do it this way, wrap the ball with foil and glue or tape it to the end of the tube. Then, cover the tube with felt and have the kids decorate it. This makes a great microphone, and the kids sang into them the rest of the party.

Ideas for what the guests can bring: music gift cards, CDs empty or full, microphones, craft supplies, or the song of their choice.

For the Risk Taker
Have the guests come ready to sing; you have songs ready, and they have to sing whatever is selected for them. You could even put the names of the songs on pieces of paper. Have each guest pick a piece of paper and then sing the song that was selected. You could also just let the kids could come up with creative ways to select who has to sing each song.

Party Favors
For Everyone
You can give them the CD that you made with party songs. By having the birthday child write "Thank you for coming" on top, it also serves as a quick thank you note.

Guests can keep their decorated CDs or microphones, if you choose to do one or both of them.

For the Risk Taker
Take lots of pictures of them performing and those can be the gift – possibly burned onto CDs with the thank you note written on them. You could also have them decorate a frame to put the picture in if that is what you want to do.

Invitations
If people are resisting your "no gifts" policy, encourage them to wrap whatever they are bringing to the party.

If you are mailing them or hand delivering them: Use card stock to create a CD or microphone shape.

Give them a blank CD to burn the song on; this would only work if you are hand delivering them. Deliver it in a case and put all the party information on the case as a label.

Cake and Food Ideas
Make a cake look like a microphone. Use a rectangle cake for the handle (you may have to cut it to slim it down) and a circle one for the top. You could also bake the cake in a glass bowl to give the top of the microphone more dimension. Ice the cake and decorate the circular top with candy coated chocolate pieces to make it stand out.

Make the cake look like a CD: circle cake with silver icing around it and a black center or cut out the center. Decorate it to look like a CD of the birthday child as the singer.

Make a brownie in the shape of a circle and turn it into a record. Very simple!

Bake cupcake mix in ice cream cones to look like microphones. You can top them with icing and put mini candy coated chocolate pieces on as well; makes the cupcakes look more like a microphone – and more delicious. Attach a red licorice string to the bottom for the wire. (To simplify even further, I used ice cream in cones and gave the kids sprinkles and candy to decorate and eat.)

This would be a good party to have them make their own pizza. Bake the dough ahead of time slightly or you can use English muffins or bagels to help simplify it for individual pizzas. Pizza sauce, cheese, and toppings set out in separate bowls make for a fun lunch the kids can make.

Games to Play
Musical Chairs
Name that Tune

Microphone dessert

 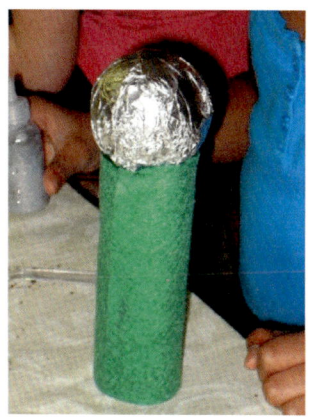

(Before)   Making microphones   (After)

Miss Pretty-Pretty Party

Fun Party Activities
For Everyone
Paint toes, paint nails, "do" make-up and hair.
Have other moms or dads stay (or ask some high school girls, your babysitter or friends) in order to play the role of beauticians. Prepare an area for the party that you are comfortable with in case of spills.

For the Risk Taker
If you are really brave and the kids are old enough, let them "do up" each other and then show it off after. Be sure to have polish, nail clippers, nail file, hairbrush, spray, hair clips, etc. If you are up for it, put out some make-up. For my daughter's party, I invited some neighbors and their moms. Each mom took a different child and made their hair fancy. Then, they soaked their feet in the tub with chairs around it and had juice in plastic champagne glasses. At the end they all sat on the couch with cucumbers on their eyes while the moms did their own child's pedicure. All the girls went home wanting to do it again and wanting their next party to be the same way. Even though it was just the moms pampering the kids, the kids still loved it.

Ideas for what the guests can bring: nail polish, nail file, nail clippers, hairspray, clips for hair, hairbrush, comb, foam rollers, curling iron, blow dryer, plastic champagne glasses, any type of spa or beauty supply.

Party Favors
For Everyone
A nail polish they did not bring.

Make a gift bag for this with a couple beauty supplies; be sure to keep it cheap and simple.

Invitations
If people are resisting your "no gifts" policy, encourage them to wrap whatever they are bringing to the party.

If you are mailing them: Pictures cut out from a magazine of women at a beauty shop.

Foil cut in a circle and glued onto card stock to look like a mirror, with information on the back.
You could even write some of the information in lipstick.

Cake and Food Ideas
Spa cake - Make two cakes: one in a loaf pan and one sheet cake. The loaf cake will be the tub and the sheet cake is the bathroom floor. Put the loaf onto the sheet cake and cover that with icing. Sticks of bubble gum can be used around the "tub" for tiles on the floor. It looks cute if you find two colors of gum and mix them up. For the tub (loaf), cover it with icing and put half a small plastic doll on the top to look like it is sitting in the tub surrounded by bubbles. Bubbles can be blue candy circles, and the person can even be made out of cookies, pretzels, etc. if you don't want to cut a plastic doll in half. My friend made this cake and took a stick of gum held on the side of the tub as a towel! Be creative, even having your child help decorate it.

Finger foods and fancy appetizers are great for this party. Sandwiches cut small or sausages wrapped in a roll make for simple party foods.

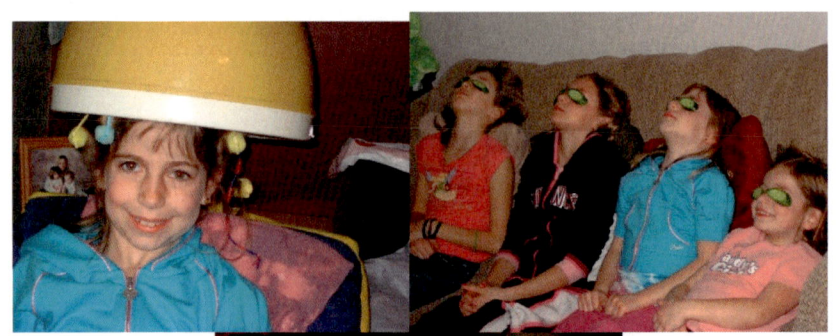

Skateboard Party

Fun Party Activities
<u>For Everyone</u>
Give everyone pre-cut pieces of wood to make their own mini skateboard ramp (balsa wood works and bends well). I would suggest getting a rectangular piece for the top and two triangular pieces for the sides. Depending on the wood you bought, wood glue should work just fine so you won't need nails. Spend time playing with learning new tricks.

Have a big homemade ramp ready for decorating.

Have guests bring skateboarding equipment (helmets and skateboards) and let them spend the afternoon skateboarding.

Ideas for what guests can bring: pieces of wood, nails, hammer, screws, screw driver, paint, sandpaper, helmet, wood glue, wheels for skateboard.

<u>For the Risk Taker</u>
Take a group of kids to a free outdoor Skate Park.

<u>For the Very Daring</u>
Make a bigger ramp together. This requires a lot of cutting, measuring, nailing, screwing and overall building. Consider pre-cutting the pieces and letting the guests put it together. After assembly, they can paint it.

Party Favors
<u>For Everyone</u>
The ramp they made with a mini skateboard to use on it.

<u>For the Risk Taker</u>
A picture of the group playing at the Skate Park or kids separately doing tricks. This can be used as the thank you card. Also, you can

go to the Skate Park and then come back to make a mini ramp for the favor.

For the Very Daring
The memories each kid will have making the ramp. Most of them will be back to use the ramp anyway. A good idea may be to give out the plans and instructions on how the ramp was made.

Invitations
If people are resisting your "no gifts" policy, encourage them to wrap whatever they are bringing to the party.

If you are mailing them: Cut a piece of sand paper into the shape of a skateboard and write the invitation information on the other side. A helpful option would be to print the information on a big label and then attach that to the back of the sandpaper skateboard.

Cake and Food Ideas
Have the kids turn Twinkies into skateboards using the Twinkies and some mini chocolate sandwich cookies as wheels.

If you want one big cake, cut rounded corners off a rectangle shaped cake, frost it and add four mini donuts to the side as the wheels. Be sure to add decoration with candy on the top of the skateboard.

Hot dogs would be a great food to have at the party and can be made to look like skateboards.

Have a big sub for all the kids to take a slice. If you are going to the park, you could even pack each kid a mini sub for them to eat at the park when they are hungry. With the right bread/buns subs could look like skateboards by attaching cucumber slices for wheels.

White Elephant Party

Fun Party Activities

<u>For Everyone</u>

Ask each person to bring a wrapped "gift" from home that they don't play with anymore. Please make sure the guests understand that they will be coming home without this "gift." Collect the gifts as they enter the party. If you have boys and girls, you may want to mark them or request that gifts are not gender specific. Determine an order the children get to select a gift to open and have them each choose a gift other than the one they brought to the party. Before the guests open gifts, remind everyone this is for fun and everyone will go home with something that might be just a silly gift.

Another fun way to decide who gets which gift is to have each guest hold the gift he or she brought. An adult or someone else not participating reads a story in which the words "left" and "right" are used often. Maybe a story about the "Left Family" that did not know right from wrong. Each time the guests hear the direction word, the gifts are passed around the circle in that direction. The game stops when the reading stops. Guests open whichever gift they are holding.

If you prefer new gifts, give a monetary limit for each kid to use to purchase a new item at that price. Wrap the "gift" and bring it to the party. Pass out numbers to each child attending. The birthday child should be first. He or she picks a present to open; the next person can take any gift that has been opened or open a new one. If the child takes something from another guest, the child who just "lost" his or her "gift" chooses and opens another still wrapped gift. At the end, the birthday child gets to pick out any of the gifts to exchange with his or hers or can keep the one he/she has at that time.

Ideas for what the guests can bring: The gift of their choice - specify whether new, in good condition from their house, something funny, or give them a theme.

Party Favors
For Everyone
The gift each child opens. This makes it easy for you to not have to worry about goodie bags, and each kid gets a new toy. I had this party for my child, and, trust me, it is great! She did not care that she only got one present, and she enjoyed watching her friends open gifts. They all had fun receiving from one another as well.

Invitations
If people are resisting your "no gifts" policy, encourage them to wrap whatever they are bringing to the party.

If you are mailing them: Any invitation will work for this party! An elephant shape or a theme could be ideal.

Cake and Food Ideas
This is a perfect party for your child to pick a favorite cake or dessert.

At my daughter's white elephant party, we served smores as the dessert. I burned a marshmallow and that was what she blew out while we sang happy birthday to her. All the guests loved it!

Have your child pick his/her favorite food and serve that. Nice and relaxed and easy. Remember, you don't have to serve a meal at every party!

Games to Play
This party can be all about FUN! Ask the birthday child what games they would like to play.
Relay Races
Water Balloon toss
"Minute to win it" competitions
Pin the tail on the elephant

Zoo Theme Party

Fun Party Activities

<u>For Everyone</u>

Each guest can bring an animal they would find at the zoo. This could be small plastic animals or stuffed animals. If you want this as the gift, suggest certain animals for each guest to bring. Give each guest some options of animals found at the zoo. As the guests arrive, they can set up and create a zoo. While the kids are setting up the zoo, have some wooden craft sticks out and shoe boxes for them to make cages for the animals.

Allow the kids to be creative. They can make tickets for people to enter the zoo and give tours. Use items around the house to create trees, water, dirt, and even some fake food for the guests to feed to the animals. When the parents pick up their kids, have birthday guests escort them and narrate a trip through the homemade zoo.

Ideas for what guests can bring: stuffed animals, small plastic animals, craft supplies, glue, tape, wooden craft sticks, shoe boxes, white shirts.

<u>For the Risk Taker</u>

Have each guest bring a white tee shirt. Have some extra t-shirts on hand in case people forget. When everyone arrives, make lion shirts with the child's hand prints. The handprints go in a circle and the face in the middle is made by fingerprints. My friend did this at her party, and it gives the kids a gift that will last. You will need orange, yellow, brown, and black paint.

<u>For the Very Daring</u>

Ask the guests that are refusing the no gift policy to adopt an animal at your local zoo. Sometimes when you do this, the child will still get a stuffed animal and a letter saying that he/she has adopted this animal. For the birthday party, you could go to the zoo or have the children set up their own zoo.

Party Favors

For Everyone

You could make sure to have enough wooden craft sticks and boxes on hand so that each guest can keep a cage for the animal they brought. You can take a picture of the group with the zoo they made behind them as the backdrop and use that as the thank you card, as well as the favor.

For the Risk Taker

The lion shirt they made.

For the Very Daring

Memories and possibly photos of guests, birthday kid, and the animals that were adopted.

Invitations

If people are resisting your "no gifts" policy, encourage them to wrap whatever they are bringing to the party.

If you are mailing them: Make the invitation look like your child's favorite animal.

Buy some inexpensive cards with animals on them. Use animal stickers to decorate any invitation.

Dress your child in an animal costume. Use the picture with the information on the back.

Make the invitation look like a ticket to the zoo.

Cake and Food Ideas

Make the cake look like your child's favorite animal. My daughter is into monkeys, so I bought a cake pan in the shape of a monkey and just used brownie mix.

Make a sheet cake and buy some plastic zoo animals or animal crackers to put on top. You can be creative by using candy or other food options to add other features you may see in the zoo.

If you plan to have a party at a time where you don't have to serve a meal, this would be a good party for that. Just serve kids some snacks similar to concessions at the zoo: popcorn, elephant ears, pretzels, animal crackers, etc.

Pay the Challenge Forward

This is an afterward for you crusaders, when you have to send a gift to a party. You can forge ahead with some creative gifts that will maintain your position of no gifts but will not offend the host.

Give anything that is a gift of time spent together
  Picnic in the park
  Day at the beach
  Trip to the sledding hill
  Movie night at your house
  Ticket to an adventure with their friend
  Take child to mini golf or other fun activity
  Game night
  Bike riding
  Trip to get ice cream

Anything you give that is a gift of service
  Walk the dog
  Help you clean your room
  Homemade Spa Day

Gifts that keep on giving
  Magazine subscription
  Adopt an animal
  Craft supplies
  Favorite games

Gifts that are *things* are so limited in scope. I hope that you will challenge yourself, not only in the parties you throw (for yourself, your friends, your children) but also in the example you set in the type of gifts you give. Just give the birthday child a printed gift certificate with what you want to do with them. Talk to the parents ahead of time and set up a date, in order to make sure the gift can happen.

This book is really not meant to eliminate gifts. I am not the Grinch! It is to show that a true gift is so much more than the latest and greatest toy. The best gifts to anyone are the gifts that last. The memories, the pictures, the time spent with loved ones, or even the big collective gift left from a party. Memorable gifts, Please!

Happy Planning!

46593321R00036

Made in the USA
Middletown, DE
04 August 2017